ideas

ideas

kitchens and dining rooms
cocinas y comedores
cuisines et salles à manger
küchen und esszimmer

AUTHORS
Fernando de Haro & Omar Fuentes

EDITORIAL DESIGN & PRODUCTION

EDITORES   PUBLISHERS

PROJECT MANAGERS
Carlos Herver Díaz
Ana Teresa Vázquez de la Mora
Laura Mijares Castellá

COORDINATION
Ana Lydia Arcelus Cano
Cristina Gutiérrez Herce
Alejandra Martínez-Báez Aldama

PREPRESS COORDINATION
José Luis de la Rosa Meléndez

COPYWRITER
Laura Carolina Bueno López

ENGLISH TRANSLATION
Fionn Petch

FRENCH TRANSLATION
Isadora Mora

GERMAN TRANSLATION
Claudia Wondratschke

Ideas
kitchens and dining rooms . cocinas y comedores
cuisines et salles à manger . küchen und esszimmer

© 2013, Fernando de Haro & Omar Fuentes

AM Editores S.A. de C.V.
Paseo de Tamarindos 400 B, suite 109, Col. Bosques de las Lomas,
C.P. 05120, México, D.F., Tel. 52(55) 5258 0279
E-mail: ame@ameditores.com   www.ameditores.com

ISBN: 978-607-437-297-7

Printed in China.

introduction   introducción

The kitchen and dining room are one of the most important spaces in the home. This almost mystical space in which food is prepared, exercises a magnetic pull over the infrastructure of a house, almost as if it were hypnotic.

The kitchen is a busy area, whether rapidly in the mornings preparing breakfast, sharing food at lunchtime, taking a snack during the day, and of course at night when the whole family meets there. With all this movement, it must be a highly practical and efficient space that enables us to maintain order and cleanliness at all times, yet without losing sight of beauty and charm.

La cocina y el comedor, son de las áreas más importantes en el hogar. Ese espacio casi místico en donde se preparan los alimentos, ejerce un efecto atrayente en los habitantes de la casa como si de hipnosis se tratara.

La cocina es muy transitada, ya sea a toda prisa en las mañanas para desayunar, por las tardes para compartir los alimentos, tomar un bocadillo durante el día y por supuesto en la noche cuando toda la familia se reúne. Con tanto movimiento, debe ser un lugar altamente práctico y eficaz que nos permita mantener el orden y la limpieza en todo momento; pero no por esto apartado de belleza y encanto.

introduction   einleitung

La cuisine et la salle à manger sont les pièces les plus importantes d'une maison. Cet espace presque mystique où les repas sont préparés attire les habitants de la maison comme par une sorte d'hypnose.

La cuisine est très fréquentée : les matins en une visite express pour le petit déjeuner, les après-midis pour partager un repas, durant la journée pour un casse-croute, bien évidemment, le soir, lorsque toute la famille se réunit. Avec tant de mouvement, la cuisine doit être ce lieu pratique et efficace nous permettant de maintenir l'ordre et l'hygiène à tout moment. Mais cela ne signifie pas qu'elle ne soit pas belle et charmante.

Küche und Esszimmer gehören zu den wichtigsten Bereichen in einem Haus. Dieser fast mystische Raum in dem Lebensmittel zubereitet werden, übt eine anziehende fast hypnotische Wirkung auf die Bewohner des Hauses auf.

Die Küche ist ein stark frequentierter Ort, entweder in Eile am Morgen zum Frühstück, mittags zum Essen, für Snacks im Laufe des Tages und natürlich abends, wenn die ganze Familie zusammenkommt. Bei so viel Bewegung sollte sie ein höchst praktischer und effizienter Ort sein, damit zu jeder Zeit Ordnung und Sauberkeit herrscht, aber gleichzeitig auch Schönheit und Charme.

The materials and decoration of kitchens should not only represent cleanliness but also share in the overall style of the house, meaning it is essential to pay attention to the finishes of shelves, cupboards and even appliances, to ensure these are both functional and ornamental at the same time.

The dining room, meanwhile, is the family hub. This space for enjoying food is the perfect excuse for spending time with family and friends, relaxing and enjoying the table talk or losing oneself in the blend of flavors. This means that a dining room needs to be both comfortable and attractive.

Whatever decorative style is chosen for the dining room, the details of lighting and the comfort of the chairs combine with the design of the table and ornaments are all essential when it comes to creating a harmonious and welcoming ambiance that enables us to enjoy a good meal.

Los materiales y decoración de las cocinas, no sólo deben representar pulcritud, también es necesario que compartan el estilo general de la casa, por lo que es imprescindible poner atención en los recubrimientos de alacenas y repisas e incluso en electrodomésticos, para que estos resulten funcionales y ornamentales al mismo tiempo.

Por su parte el comedor es justamente el punto de reunión familiar. Ese espacio en el que degustar los alimentos se convierte en el pretexto perfecto para compartir con la familia y amigos, relajarse y disfrutar de una agradable sobremesa o simplemente perderse en la mezcla de sabores. Por esta razón, el comedor debe ser cómodo, confortable y hermoso al mismo tiempo.

Sea cual sea el estilo decorativo que se escoja en el comedor, los detalles en la iluminación y el confort de los asientos, sumándose al diseño de la mesa y ornamentos serán esenciales al momento de crear una

Les matériaux et la décoration des cuisines ne doivent pas uniquement nous permettre de maintenir l'hygiène, ils doivent accompagner le style de toute la maison. Prêtez attention aux recouvrements des placards et des étagères, et même aux électroménagers, car ils doivent être aussi beaux que fonctionnels.

La salle à manger, c'est le point de ralliement de la famille. Ce le lieu où la dégustation d'un repas n'est qu'une excuse pour retrouver la famille et les amis, se détendre, profiter d'un agréable moment pousse-café ou tout simplement profiter d'un mélange de saveurs pour le palais. La salle à manger doit être aussi belle que confortable.

Indépendamment de la décoration, l'éclairage, des sièges confortables et le style de la table sont des éléments non négligeables au moment de concevoir une atmosphère chaleureuse nous permettant de profiter d'un bon repas.

Die Materialien und die Dekoration der Küche sollten nicht nur Sauberkeit ausstrahlen, sondern auch den gesamten Stil des Hauses teilen. Hierbei ist es wichtig, auf die Verkleidung der Schränke, Regale und sogar der Küchengeräte zu achten, damit diese funktional und gleichzeitig schön anzusehen sind.

Das Esszimmer hingegen ist der Ort, wo sich die Familie trifft. Dieser Raum wo gegessen wird, ist perfekt, um mit der Familie und Freunden zusammen zu kommen, sich zu entspannen, diverse Speisen zu genießen oder um sich einfach in der Mischung von Aromen zu verlieren. Aus diesem Grund sollte dieses Zimmer komfortabel, bequem und zugleich schön anzusehen sein.

Welchen dekorativen Stil man für das Esszimmer auch wählt, welche Details in der Beleuchtung und bezüglich des Sitzkomforts, sie sollten das Design des Tischs und der Verzierungen ergänzen und sind entscheidend für eine harmonische und warme Atmosphäre, die erlaubt hier eine gute Mahlzeit zu genießen.

The kitchen and dining room are usually located close to each other to help with food service, although recently the kitchen has acquired greater importance as a place for the family to come together. As a result, it is usual to find breakfast bars and islands forming part of the kitchen's layout, accessories that come in all kinds of sizes, shapes and materials, whether square, round, oval, double-decked, and in glass, granite, or marble. What matters is that they suit the overall design of the kitchen, and help to make it a more dynamic, pleasant and functional space.

When harmony and balance is found between kitchen and dining room, this helps to transmit the image, design and style of our personality when it comes to showing off and sharing our home.

atmósfera armoniosa y cálida, que permita disfrutar de una buena comida.

La cocina y el comedor suelen ubicarse en áreas cercanas de la casa para la fácil distribución de alimentos, pero ya no es sólo por eso, en la actualidad la cocina ha tomado una mayor importancia en la convivencia familiar, por eso no es de extrañar que amplios desayunadores y cómodas barras o islas formen parte de la estructura en la cocina; estos accesorios se encuentran en todo tipo de tamaños, formas y materiales, pueden ser cuadradas, circulares, ovaladas, de doble tablero, de cristal, granito, mármol, etc. Lo importante es que sean acordes con el diseño general de la cocina, para hacer este espacio más dinámico, agradable y funcional.

Cuando se obtiene concordancia y equilibrio entre cocina y comedor, se logra transmitir la imagen, diseño y estilo, conforme a nuestra personalidad, al momento de lucir y compartir el hogar.

Cuisine et salle à manger sont souvent des pièces voisines afin de faciliter la distribution du repas. Mais ce n'est plus la seule raison. Des nos jours, les cuisines sont davantage importantes car elles encouragent la vie familiale. Il n'est point étonnant d'y trouver des bars et des dessertes. Ils existent dans toutes les tailles, formes et type de matériaux. Ils sont carrés, rondes, ovales, en verre, en granit, en marbre... Mais surtout, ces éléments accompagnent la décoration de la cuisine, afin que celle-ci soit dynamique, agréable et fonctionnelle.

Lorsque entre la salle à manger et la cuisine règne l'harmonie, notre personnalité y est reflétée. Cela est perceptible pendant les moments de convivialité.

Die Küche und Esszimmer befinden sich in der Regel in einem Haus in der Nähe damit das Essen einfach verteilt werden kann. Das ist heute nicht mehr nur aus diesem Grund der Fall. Die Küche hat inzwischen eine wichtigere Rolle im Familienleben eingenommen. Daher ist es nicht verwunderlich, dass breite Frühstückstische und komfortable Bars oder Inseln Teil der Struktur einer Küche geworden sind. Diese gibt es in allen Größen, Formen und Materialien. Sie können quadratisch, rund, oval, von doppelter Länge, aus Glas, Granit, Marmor, etc. sein. Das Wichtigste ist, dass sie sich im Einklang mit dem Gesamtkonzept der Küche befinden, um diesen Bereich dynamischer, angenehmer und funktionaler zu machen.

Wenn zwischen der Küche und dem Essbereich Übereinstimmung und Gleichgewicht herrscht, kann durch sie während des Gebrauchs ein Bild, ein Design und ein Stil vermittelt werden, der unserer Persönlichkeit entspricht.

eclectic
eclécticas
éclectique
eklektisch

shared spaces
ambientes compartidos
pièces communes
gemeinschaftsräume

WITH THEIR BREADTH AND LIGHT, shared spaces are an excellent way of unifying the home. It is important to bear in mind that eclectic decoration comprises a fusion of styles, meaning the objective is to integrate elements of color, function, texture, form and weight, while ensuring the space does not appear confusing. To avoid this, use similar materials for the floor, ceiling or windows, or ornamental objects.

POR SU AMPLITUD Y LUMINOSIDAD, los espacios compartidos son una excelente opción que unifica el hogar. Es importante tener en cuenta que la decoración ecléctica consiste en una fusión de estilos, por lo que el objetivo es integrar elementos de color, función, textura, forma y peso procurando que el espacio no se vea confuso, para esto se puede recurrir a homologar materiales en piso, techo, ventanales o artículos ornamentales.

SPACIEUSES ET LUMINEUSES, les pièces communes sont une excellente option pour unifier une maison. La décoration éclectique consiste à fusionner les différents styles, le but est d'intégrer couleurs, fonctions, textures, formes et poids. L'espace doit néanmoins rester dégagé. Pour ce faire, il faudrait unifier le sol, le plafond, le toit, les verrières et les objets décoratifs.

AUFGRUND IHRER GERÄUMIGKEIT UND HELLIGKEIT sind Gemeinschaftsräume eine ausgezeichnete Möglichkeit, um ein Heim zu vereinheitlichen. Dabei sollte man beachten, dass die eklektische Dekoration aus einer Fusion von unterschiedlichen Stilen besteht, deren Ziel es ist, farbige und funktionale Elemente, Textur, Form und Gewicht zu integrieren, ohne dass der Raum konfus wirkt. Dies kann man erreichen, indem man die Materialen des Fußbodens mit denen der Decke, der Fenster und der Dekorationsgegenstände vereinheitlicht.

HARMONIZING SHARED SPACES is very important and can be achieved by maintaining the same floor covering throughout to give continuity. If coverings are used in the kitchen in a similar range of colors to the dining room table and chairs, this emphasizes the balance between the two spaces. To finish off, decorative details like plants and flowers will complete the harmony of the space.

LA UNIFICACIÓN EN LOS AMBIENTES COMPARTIDOS es muy importante, para lograrlo es recomendable utilizar el mismo piso dándole continuidad al ambiente. Si se colocan recubrimientos en la cocina en una gama similar a la mesa y las sillas del comedor, se realza el equilibrio entre los dos espacios. Por último, algunos detalles decorativos como plantas y flores, completarán la armonía del lugar.

L'INTÉGRATION DES ESPACES PARTAGÉS est très importante. Il convient d'unifier le recouvrement au sol pour favoriser la continuité de cette pièce. Nous pouvons retrouver un équilibre lorsque les recouvrements pour la cuisine, la table et les chaises de la salle à manger ont une apparence uniforme. Quelques objets décoratifs —des plantes, des fleurs— viennent compéter l'harmonie de cette pièce.

DIESE VEREINHEITLICHUNG VON GEMEINSCHAFTSRÄUMEN ist sehr wichtig. Am besten funktioniert das, indem man den gleichen Boden verwendet und dadurch der Umgebung eine gewisse Kontinuität gibt. Die Verkleidungen in der Küche sollten eine ähnliche Farbpalette wie der Tisch und die Stühle des Esszimmers haben, dadurch entsteht ein Gleichgewicht zwischen den beiden Räumen. Schließlich vollenden einige dekorative Details wie Pflanzen und Blumen die Harmonie des Raums.

In large communal areas that share a lounge, dining room and kitchen, the unification and harmony of the whole is important. Using similar finishes for floors and ceiling throughout, and the use of two contrasting tones that interweave as the primary combination in furnishings and walls provides a sense of unity to the space. Finally, furnishing the kitchen with a practical open bar highlights and merges the spaces.

En áreas comunes amplias que comparten sala, comedor y cocina, la unificación y armonía del conjunto es importante. Homogenizar acabados en pisos y techos por todo el lugar y el uso de dos tonalidades de contraste, que se entrelacen como combinación primaria en mobiliario y muros, brindan una sensación de unidad en el ambiente. Por último, dejar la cocina con una práctica barra abierta resalta y fusiona los espacios.

Dans les grandes pièces communes où nous retrouvons le salon, la salle à manger, et la cuisine, l'uniformité et l'harmonie sont importantes. Les finitions des sols et des plafonds doivent être uniformes. Le mobilier et les murs doivent utiliser deux couleurs qui vont se contraster. Finalement, un plan de travail dans la cuisine permet de distinguer chacun des espaces, et de les fondre en même temps.

In großzügigen Gemeinschaftsräumen, wie Wohnzimmer, Esszimmer und Küche ist die Vereinheitlichung und Harmonie aller Bereiche sehr wichtig. Die Homogenisierung von Fußböden und Decken und der Einsatz von zwei kontrastierenden Farben, die sich in Möbeln und Wänden miteinander verflechten, schaffen ein Gefühl der Einheit. Wird die Küche mit einer praktischen offenen Bar versehen, wirkt diese als Verbindungsglied der unterschiedlichen Bereiche.

A clear, uniform color for the walls fosters an effective but discreet fusion between dining room and kitchen, and also helps to place the emphasis on tables made from tinted wood. Adding a bar between the spaces delimits the different areas without intruding on the gaze.

Una tonalidad clara y uniforme en los muros propicia una eficaz pero discreta fusión entre comedor y cocina; además ayudará a resaltar cualquier mesa de madera entintada. Si se añade una barra entre los espacios se logra delimitar el área sin cortar la vista.

Des murs clairs et uniformes permettent de fondre salle à manger et cuisine, mettant en avant une table en bois. Un bar entre les deux espaces permet de diviser la pièce sans gêner la vue.

Eine klare und einheitliche Farbe der Wände sorgt für eine wirkungsvolle aber unaufdringliche Fusion zwischen Esszimmer und Küche. Außerdem hebt sie jeden farbigen Holztisch hervor. Wenn eine Bar zwischen beiden Räumen eingesetzt wird, können beide Bereiche abgegrenzt werden, ohne dabei die Sicht zu versperren.

bars and dining tables
barras y comedores
bars et salles à manger
bars und esstische

THE DECORATION OF THE DINING ROOM focuses on the choice of table: whether large and classical or rustic and irregular, in combination with the chairs it forms the central point of the room. Naturally, lighting is essential to the ambiance, helping to emphasize textures and fostering the right atmosphere to share and enjoy food.

LA DECORACIÓN DE LA ESTANCIA COMEDOR se centra principalmente en la elección de la mesa, ya sea grande y de corte clásico o de madera rústica y disforme, la mesa en combinación con las sillas será el punto central de nuestra habitación. Por supuesto que la iluminación será indispensable en la ambientación del lugar, ayudando a resaltar las texturas y propiciando la atmósfera adecuada para compartir y disfrutar los alimentos.

POUR DÉCORER LA SALLE À MANGER il faut tout d'abord choisir la table : grande et classique ; en bois, rustique et difforme ; etc. Table et chaises sont au cœur de la pièce. L'éclairage est indispensable pour reproduire une ambiance, il met en avant les textures et recrée une ambiance propice pour partager un repas.

DIE DEKORATION DES ESSZIMMERS konzentriert sich vor allem auf die Wahl des Esstisches. Ob groß und klassisch geschnitten oder aus rustikalem Holz und verformt, ist der Tisch in Kombination mit Stühlen der Mittelpunkt unseres Raumes. Natürlich ist auch die Beleuchtung unverzichtbar und hilft die Strukturen des Raumes hervorzuheben und die richtige Atmosphäre für den Genuss gemeinsamen Essens zu schaffen.

GRANITE BAR TOPS in combination with wooden furniture make for a pleasant, conventional setting. If the effect sought is a traditional space with modern touches, the ideal composition may be found in a large slab of wood —whether natural or varnished— and dark metal chairs.

LAS BARRAS CON CUBIERTAS EN GRANITO en combinación con mobiliario de madera resultan en un ambiente agradable y convencional. Si lo que se busca es un entorno rústico con detalles de modernidad, la composición ideal se encuentra en un tablón de madera, ya sea natural o barnizado, y sillas metálicas en color obscuro.

AVEC DES BARS EN GRANIT combinés à un mobilier en bois, vous pouvez recréer une ambiance agréable et conventionnelle. Si vous cherchez une déco rustique avec une touche moderne, prenez un bar en bois —naturel ou verni— et combinez-le avec des chaises métalliques en couleur foncée.

MIT GRANIT VERKLEIDETE BARS in Kombination mit Holzmöbeln schaffen ein angenehmes und konventionelles Ambiente. Wenn man einen rustikalen Stil mit modernen Details vorzieht, ist die ideale Zusammensetzung ein Holzbrett, ob natürlich oder lackiert, und Metallstühle in dunkler Farbe.

Brick walls and a rustic wooden bar top suggest a special, welcoming space. The black cladding around the base of the bar and the chair seats endow the grouping with a sophisticated, masculine feel.

Las paredes en ladrillo y la barra de madera rústica hacen un espacio único y acogedor. El revestimiento negro en la base de la barra y el asiento de las sillas consiguen que además el conjunto luzca sofisticado y masculino.

Des murs en briques et un plan de travail en bois rustique font de cet espace un endroit unique et chaleureux. Un même recouvrement noir pour la base du plan de travail et pour l'assise des chaises donne à cet ensemble un aspect masculin et sophistiqué.

Die Wände aus Backstein und die Bar aus rustikalem Holz schaffen einen einzigartigen und gemütlichen Raum. Die schwarze Verkleidung am Fuß der Bar und am Sitz der Stühle, sorgt dafür, dass die Kombination raffiniert und männlich aussieht.

If the aim is for the visual stimulus of the room to be a deep, saturated color, the best option is to complement this with a measure of neutral and discreet tones that serve to emphasize the compositional balance of color.

Si se desea que el estímulo visual de la estancia recaiga en un tono intenso y saturado, lo ideal es complementarlo con la mesura de tonos neutros y discretos que resalten el equilibrio compositivo del color.

Si vous souhaitez qu'une couleur vive et saturée soit le stimulus visuel, compensez-le avec des couleurs neutres et discrètes afin de restaurer l'équilibre dans la palette de couleurs.

Wenn man möchte, dass der visuelle Reiz des Raumes ein tiefer und gesättigter Farbton sein soll, kombiniert man diesen idealerweise mit neutralen und gedämpften Tönen, die die kompositorische Balance der Farben hervorhebt.

An alliance can be formed between furnishings with different finishes, such as rustic wood, metal or tinted maple wood, if a few
ornamental touches of classic figurines and blocks of intense color
are used to provide balance to the whole.

Se puede lograr una alianza entre mobiliario con distintos acabados como: madera rústica, metálicos o tintes de madera maple,
si se añaden algunos toques ornamentales de figurillas clásicas y
paños con colores intensos que le den equilibrio al conjunto.

Nous pouvons établir une alliance entre le mobilier et les finitions
en bois rustique, métal ou bois d'érable. Pour retrouver un équilibre,
ajoutez des objets décoratifs comme des petites sculptures et chiffons
en couleurs intenses.

Eine Vereinigung verschiedenartiger Möbel aus rustikalem Holz, Me-
tall oder farbigen Ahornholz kann erreicht werden, wenn man Verzierungen wie klassische Figuren und Bezüge mit intensiven Farben
hinzufügt, die dem Ganzen ein gewisses Gleichgewicht verleihen.

A dining room in a beach home cultivates an ambience of greater freedom and relaxation, and favors the use of woven textures for the chairs, which provoke a sensation of pleasure evoking the natural world. Complete the decoration with deep colors and organic textures to generate the right atmosphere.

Un comedor en una casa de playa propicia un ambiente más libre y relajado por lo que el uso de tejidos o entramados en las sillas es recomendable, ya que provocan una sensación de placidez evocando lo natural. Completar la decoración con colores saturados y texturas orgánicas genera el ambiente adecuado.

Le style d'une salle à manger dans une maison à la plage est beaucoup plus libre et décontracté. Il convient d'utiliser des chaises habillées en toile ou tressées pour plus de plaisir et pour un contact avec la nature. Utilisez des couleurs saturées et des textures organiques pour compléter la décoration.

Ein Esszimmer in einem Strandhaus schafft eine freiere und entspanntere Atmosphäre. Daher wird die Verwendung von Stühlen aus gewebten Stoff oder Korbstühle empfohlen, da sie ein Gefühl der Ruhe und Natürlichkeit vermitteln. Die Dekoration wird mit sanften Farben und organischen Texturen vervollständigt und schafft damit eine angenehme Atmosphäre.

kitchens with islands
cocinas con isla
cuisines avec dessertes
küchen mit inseln

THE FUNCTIONALITY of islands in kitchens cannot be overstated. Their utility lies in their ability to expand the space, whether used as a breakfast bar, support table, or to contain the hob. They can take different shapes, sizes and finishes that allow them to combine with the general decoration of the home, whether to blend in or to create a more intimate and comfortable space. Creating an island is not only convenient, but also establishes a beautiful homely ambience.

LA FUNCIONALIDAD de las islas en la cocina es innegable, su utilidad radica en ampliar el espacio, ya sea como desayunador, mesa de apoyo, estufa, etc. Existen en distintas formas, tamaños y texturas, lo que permite combinarlas con la decoración general del hogar, ya sea homogenizándola o creando un ambiente más íntimo y confortable. Contar con una isla no sólo es conveniente, además proporcionan un entorno bellamente hogareño.

NOUS NE POUVONS pas nier qu'une desserte est très pratique en cuisine. Il nous fait gagner de la place, il remplit la fonction d'une table, d'un plan de travail, d'un support pour la table de cuisson... Elle existe dans toutes les formes, tailles et textures, ce qui permet de l'assortir facilement à la décoration de toute la maison. Elle nous permet de recréer une atmosphère plus intime et confortable. Une desserte n'est pas uniquement pratique, elle fait d'un foyer un endroit chaleureux.

DIE FUNKTIONALITÄT von Inseln in der Küche ist nicht zu leugnen, ihre Nützlichkeit liegt in der Ausweitung des Raums, sei es ihr Nutzen als Frühstückstisch, Arbeitstisch, Herd, usw. Es gibt sie in verschiedenen Formen, Größen und mit unterschiedlichen Texturen. Das ermöglicht es, sie mit der allgemeinen Dekoration des Hauses zu kombinieren, indem man sie entweder vereinheitlicht oder eine intime und gemütliche Atmosphäre schafft. Über eine Insel zu verfügen ist nicht nur praktisch, sie sorgt auch für ein wunderschönes häusliches Ambiente.

The use of marble for worktops in the kitchen produces a sense of exquisite refinement. As well as being a fine material, it is easy to combine, due to the variety of existing colors such as black, brown, white, cream and gray. The island is the focal point of the decoration and of an ideal size to function as an eating or food preparation area. It establishes an equilibrium within the context, balancing the two zones, while the wood finish to the furniture lends itself to the indirect lighting, producing a homely effect.

El mármol como recubrimiento en la cocina produce un entorno de refinada exquisitez. Además de ser un material muy limpio, es altamente combinable debido a la variedad de colores existentes como negro, café, blanco, crema y gris. La isla es el punto central de decoración, su tamaño resulta práctico para ser usada como antecomedor o barra de tareas, se enlaza en equilibrio con todo el entorno combinando ambas cubiertas, mientras que el revestimiento de madera en el mobiliario, se presta para armonizar con luces indirectas que brindan un efecto confortable.

Le marbre, en tant que recouvrement, dégage une atmosphère exquise et raffinée. C'est, de surcroit, un matériau très hygiénique et, grâce à la diversité de couleurs —noir, marron, blanc, beige et gris— il est très facile de l'assortir. La desserte est au cœur de la décoration. Grâce à sa taille nous pouvons nous en servir en tant que plan de travail et elle se fond facilement avec le reste des éléments de cuisine. Quant au bois, il permet d'harmoniser la lumière indirecte et dégage une atmosphère de confort.

Marmor als Verkleidung in der Küche erzeugt ein Ambiente von raffinierter Exklusivität. Abgesehen davon, dass es ein sehr sauberes Material ist, ist es auch vielseitig kombinierbar aufgrund der Variation seiner Farben wie Schwarz, Braun, Weiß, Creme und Grau. Die Insel ist der Mittelpunkt der Einrichtung, ihre Größe ist praktisch, da sie als Frühstücksbereich oder Arbeitstisch verwendet werden kann. Sie verbindet sich mit der ganzen Umgebung und kombiniert beide Ablagen, während die Holzverkleidung der Möbel mit angenehmer indirekter Beleuchtung die Umgebung harmonisiert.

THE RANGE OF ORANGES is popularly associated with food, so it is very successfully used in the kitchen; its warm, vibrant tones suggest a lively, bright and cheerful atmosphere. However, it is essential to relax the visual weight with a more neutral tone in certain elements like the worktop of the island and wall tiles.

LA GAMA DE NARANJAS se asocia popularmente con los alimentos, por lo que resulta muy acertado utilizarlo en la cocina. Al tratarse de tonos cálidos y vibrantes se sugiere un ambiente vivaz, luminoso y alegre; sin embargo, es imprescindible relajar el peso visual con un tono más neutro en ciertos elementos como la cubierta de la isla y el azulejo de la pared.

LA COULEUR ORANGE est communément associée à la nourriture, c'est une bonne idée d'y penser pour la cuisine. C'est une couleur chaude et vive qui va dégager une atmosphère vivante, lumineuse et joyeuse. Cependant, il faudra contrecarrer le poids visuel avec une couleur plus neutre pour la surface de la desserte ou pour le carrelage au mur.

ORANGENE FARBTÖNE werden normalerweise mit Lebensmitteln assoziiert. Daher erscheint es durchaus angebracht, sie in der Küche zu verwenden. Diese warmen und pulsierenden Farbtöne verleihen dem Raum eine lebendige, helle und freundliche Atmosphäre. Allerdings ist es wichtig, das visuelle Gewicht mit einem neutralen Farbton bestimmter Elemente wie der Tischplatte der Insel und den Wandfliesen zu entspannen.

contemporary
contemporáneas
contemporaines
zeitgenössisch

shared spaces
ambientes compartidos
pièces communes
gemeinschaftsräume

THE PRINCIPAL OBJECTIVE of contemporary decoration is to create open and spacious areas in an atmosphere of distinction, so the use of shared spaces is an option worth considering. To give a touch of understated elegance it is advisable to use a color palette of light earth tones and discreet accessories. Furnishings are simple designs and fine lines, while the spaces are unified through the use of homogenized materials.

EL OBJETIVO PRINCIPAL de la decoración contemporánea es contar con áreas abiertas y amplias en un ambiente de distinción, por lo que el uso de ambientes compartidos es una opción adecuada. Para darle ese toque de sutil elegancia es recomendable utilizar una paleta cromática de tonos claros a térreos y accesorios discretos. Los muebles son de diseños simples y líneas finas. Los espacios se unifican a través del uso de materiales homogenizados.

LA DÉCORATION contemporaine vise à procurer des pièces tout aussi ouvertes et spacieuses qu'élégantes. C'est donc une bonne idée d'avoir des pièces communes. Pour une touche d'élégance, pensez aux couleurs claires, voir terre, et aux accessoires discrets. Des meubles avec un design très simple et des fines lignes. Nous pouvons unifier les espaces lorsque nous utilisons des matériaux homogènes.

DAS HAUPTZIEL von moderner Einrichtungen sind offene und großzügige Räume in einer distinguierten Atmosphäre, so dass die Verwendung von Gemeinschaftsräumen eine angebrachte Option darstellt. Um ihnen diesen Hauch an Eleganz zu verleihen, sollte eine Farbpalette von hellen Erdtönen und diskrete Accessoires verwendet werden. Die Möbel sind von schlichtem feinem Design. Die Räume werden durch die Verwendung von homogenisierten Materialien vereinheitlicht.

To achieve a chromatic organization that delimits each area with harmony, a contrasting floor may be used to unify the space, combining it with earth tones in the furniture, creating a warm and balanced atmosphere. Adding a rug produces a visual shock that breaks with the monochrome floor.

Para lograr una organización cromática que delimite cada área con armonía, puede utilizarse un piso de contraste que unifique y combinarlo con tonos térreos en los muebles, creando una atmósfera cálida y equilibrada. Añadir una alfombrilla, produce un choque visual que rompe la monocromía del piso.

Afin de délimiter chaque espace avec une gamme de couleurs, le sol peut vous aider à contraster et unifier. Combinez-le avec des meubles en couleurs terre pour créer une atmosphère chaleureuse et équilibrée. Ajoutez un tapis pour rompre avec le style monochrome du sol.

Um eine farbliche Ordnung herzustellen, die jeden Bereich harmonisch voneinander abgrenzt, kann man einen kontrastreichen Boden verwenden, der vereinheitlicht und diesen mit erdfarbenen Tönen der Möbel kombinieren. Dadurch wird eine warme und ausgeglichene Atmosphäre erzeugt. Ein Teppich bricht mit der Monochromie des Bodens.

If you have the space for a terrace, smooth and polished stones in contrast with rustic wood and touches of wrought iron evoke the natural elements, creating an atmosphere of relaxation.

Si se cuenta con el espacio para hacer una terraza, las piedras lisas y pulidas en contraste con madera rústica y algunos toques de herrería evocan lo natural, generando un ambiente de relajación.

Si vous avez de la place pour installer une terrasse, les pierres lisses et polies, contrastées au bois rustique et des détails en fer forgé rappellent la nature et dégagent une atmosphère détendue.

Wenn man über eine Terrasse verfügt, sind glatte und polierte Steine im Kontrast zu rustikalem Holz und einem Hauch von Eisen zu empfehlen. Diese betonen die Natürlichkeit und schaffen eine entspannte Atmosphäre.

Black and white are the ultimate expression of contrast and elegance. Their characteristics mean each has a specific function: white casts light and opens up spaces while black breaks with the highlights, adjusting the brightness of the surroundings.

Blanco y negro son la máxima expresión del contraste y la elegancia. Por sus características cada uno cumple una función específica: el blanco proyecta luz y amplía los espacios mientras que el negro rompe con la brillantez adecuando la luminosidad del entorno.

Le blanc et le noir sont l'expression du contraste et de l'élégance, par excellence. Chaque couleur rempli une fonction très spécifique : le blanc projette la lumière et agrandi les espaces ; le noir sert à contrecarrer l'éclat et la luminosité.

Schwarz und Weiß sind der ultimative Ausdruck von Kontrast und Eleganz. Aufgrund ihrer Eigenschaften erfüllt jede einzelne Farbe eine spezielle Funktion: Weiß projiziert Licht und weitet Räume, während Schwarz mit leuchtenden Farben bricht und die Helligkeit der Umgebung reguliert.

bars and dining tables
barras y comedores
bars et salles à manger
bars und esstische

THE SHAPE of the dining room is about the structural dynamics of the house, but is also influenced by the user's personality. Circular dining tables allow for wide-ranging conversation between all diners, besides the adaptation of the space. A rectangular room is more conventional and suits a hierarchical structure in the home; whereas square dining rooms optimize space and provide generous room for each diner.

LA FORMA del comedor tiene que ver con la dinámica estructural de la casa aunque también influye la personalidad del usuario. Los comedores circulares permiten una amplia relación entre todos los comensales además de la adecuación de los espacios. Un comedor rectangular resulta más convencional y adecuado para una estructura jerárquica en el hogar; mientras que los cuadrados optimizan espacios y dan amplitud a cada comensal.

LA FORME des tables pour la salle à manger répond à la structure de la maison et aux goûts de l'habitant. Les tables rondes s'adaptent à l'espace disponible et encouragent l'échange entre tous les convives. Une table rectangulaire est plus conventionnelle et répond mieux à une famille qui apprécie la hiérarchie. Les tables carrées, au contraire, rentabilisent l'espace, les convives y trouvent beaucoup plus d'espace.

DIE FORM des Esstisches hat mit der strukturellen Dynamik des Hauses zu tun, obwohl auch die Persönlichkeit des Benutzers Einfluss hat. Runde Tische ermöglichen eine breitere Kommunikation zwischen allen Tischgenossen. Ein rechteckiger Tisch ist konventioneller und für eine hierarchische Struktur im Haus geeignet. Quadratische Tische optimieren Räume und lassen jedem Tischgenossen mehr Platz.

A table in dark hues breaks with the monochromatic neutral tones around it, allowing it to stand out as the focal point of the room. Placing a mirror always helps to endow a room with a sense of spaciousness.

Una mesa en tonalidades obscuras rompe con la monocromía de los tonos neutros a su alrededor, permitiéndole destacar como punto central de la estancia. El colocar un espejo, siempre ayuda a dar sensación de amplitud.

Une table aux couleurs foncées rompt avec le style monochrome des couleurs neutres qui l'entourent. La table est ainsi au cœur de la pièce. Une glace renforcera la sensation d'espace.

Ein Tisch in dunklen Farbtönen durchbricht die monochromatisch neutralen Töne der Umgebung und hebt sich damit als Mittelpunkt des Raumes hervor. Spiegel helfen immer, einem Raum Weite zu verleihen.

Elegance and distinction are beautifully displayed in these dining rooms. Whether it is classic or modern furniture, the color black stands out and suggests a spirit of sobriety. It is advisable to choose a single decorative element that focuses attention without saturating the space.

La elegancia y distinción se encuentra bellamente representada en estos comedores. Ya sea con muebles clásicos o modernos es el negro que resalta con el entorno lo que le da el espíritu de sobriedad. Es recomendable elegir un solo elemento decorativo que focalice la atención sin saturarlo.

Ces salles à manger sont élégantes et distinguées. Qu'il s'agisse de meubles classiques ou modernes, le noir se détache du fond et apporte une touche de sobriété. Il convient de placer un seul objet décoratif afin que celui-ci accapare l'attention du regard, sans le blaser.

Diese Esstische sind gleichzeitig elegant und distinguiert. Ob mit klassischen oder modernen Möbeln, Schwarz sticht aus der Umgebung heraus und sorgt für eine gewisse Nüchternheit. Es empfiehlt sich nur ein dekoratives Element zu verwenden, das die Aufmerksamkeit auf sich zieht und das nicht übersättigt wirken sollte.

Wooden tables in very light shades, matched with surroundings that maintain the color palette of whites and creams, can generate the perception of refinement and tranquility.

Las mesas de madera en tonos muy claros, fusionadas con un entorno que se mantenga en la paleta cromática de blancos y cremas, pueden generar la percepción de limpieza y tranquilidad.

Avec des tables en bois aux couleurs très claires, combinées au blanc et beiges, la pièce projette propreté et calme.

Holztische in sehr hellen Farbtönen, die mit der Umgebung verschmelzen, die in weißen und cremefarben Tönen gehalten wird, können einen Eindruck von Sauberkeit und Ruhe vermitteln.

WHEN CHOOSING A LARGE WORK OF ART as a starting point for decoration of a dining room, it is advisable to match all the elements around it. Thus, the choice of chairs, tablecloths, centerpieces, mats and the table itself should present a subtle harmony with the colors of the painting. This provides unity to the room and serves to naturally highlight the canvas.

AL ELEGIR UNA OBRA DE ARTE de grandes dimensiones, como punto de partida de la decoración del comedor, es recomendable combinar todos los elementos alrededor de ella. Así, la elección de sillas, manteles, centros de mesa, alfombrillas y la mesa misma deberán tener una sutil armonía con las tonalidades de la pintura. De esta manera se consigue dar unidad a la estancia y resaltar de manera natural el lienzo.

LORSQUE NOUS CHOISISSONS UN GRAND TABLEAU comme partie central de la décoration d'une salle à manger, il convient d'assortir aux couleurs du tableau : chaises, sets de table, décorations de table, tapis, et même, la table. C'est ainsi que nous pouvons instaurer l'harmonie et mettre en avant le tableau.

BEI DER AUSWAHL EINES GROSSFLÄCHIGEN Kunstwerkes als Mittelpunkt der Dekoration, ist es ratsam alle Elemente auf dieses abzustimmen. Daher sollte die Auswahl der Stühle, der Tischdecken, des Tischschmucks, der Teppiche und des Tisches selber in subtiler Harmonie mit den Farben des Gemäldes stehen. So lässt sich der Raum vereinheitlichen und unterstreicht es auf natürliche Art und Weise.

kitchens with islands
cocinas con isla
cuisines avec dessertes
küchen mit inseln

WOOD used for the kitchen island sets the tone for the overall atmosphere of the room. Light colors (honey, maple or natural wood) favor a relaxed and less formal atmosphere and benefit the lighting; a straight grain and matt varnish creates a modern atmosphere. Warm reddish tints like cedar, mahogany or cherry better suit rustic kitchens with a cozy atmosphere; while dark tones like oak, walnut or ebony give a touch of sobriety and elegance.

LA MADERA, como revestimiento de la isla, construye la atmósfera general del lugar. Los tonos claros (miel, maple o natural) propician un ambiente relajado y menos formal ayudando con la iluminación; si se tienen vetas rectas y barnizadas en mate se crea un ambiente moderno. Tintes cálidos rojizos como cedro, caoba o cerezo armonizan en cocinas rústicas con un ambiente acogedor; mientras que gamas obscuras como roble, nogal o ébano dan el toque de sobriedad y elegancia.

LE BOIS, en tant que recouvrement pour la surface d'une desserte, établit l'atmosphère de la pièce. Les couleurs claires (miel, érable ou naturelle) répandent l'éclairage et instaurent une atmosphère détendue et informelle. Les bois aux veines droites et au vernis mat évoquent une atmosphère moderne. Les couleurs chaudes et rouges, comme celles du cèdre, de l'acajou ou du cerisier, sont un bon choix pour les cuisines rustiques et chaleureuses. Les couleurs foncées comme celles du chêne, du noyer ou de l'ébène, évoquent l'élégance et la sobriété.

HOLZ als Verkleidung der Insel prägt die allgemeine Atmosphäre des Ortes. Helle Farben (Honig, Ahorn oder Natur) begünstigen eine entspannte und weniger formelle Atmosphäre und machen den Raum heller. Wenn das Holz gerade gemasert und matt lackiert ist, sorgt es für ein modernes Ambiente. Warme rötliche Farbtöne wie Zeder, Mahagoni oder Kirsche harmonisieren in rustikalen Küchen mit einer gemütlichen Atmosphäre, während dunkle Holztöne wie Eiche, Nussbaum oder Ebenholz einen Hauch von Schlichtheit und Eleganz verleihen.

An island with a harmoniously matching bar grants the user a feeling of comfort and refinement. Besides its functionality, it allows for a combination of materials and tones that makes it look totally avant-garde.

Una isla con barra armoniosamente fusionada, obsequia al usuario la sensación de confort y limpieza. Además de su funcionalidad permite la combinación de materiales y tonos, haciéndola lucir totalmente vanguardista.

Une desserte avec un plan de travail attaché permet de cuisiner en toute propreté et confort. En plus d'être utile, la desserte s'assortit à tous types de matériaux et couleurs. Il n'y a pas de doute qu'il s'agit d'un élément avant-gardiste.

Eine Insel, die harmonisch mit einer Bar verbunden ist, vermittelt ihrem Benutzer das Gefühl von Komfort und Sauberkeit. Neben ihrer Funktionalität ermöglicht sie die Kombination von Materialien und Farbtönen, die sie sehr avantgardistisch erscheinen lässt.

urban
urbanas
urbaines
städtisch

IN THE CASE OF URBAN DÉCOR, shared spaces are defined by different textures and bold contrasts, expanding the palette. They use a modern and colorful decoration that stands out in each space and allows for the use of unconventional and daring materials; however, attention must always be paid to space, ample lighting and harmony with the surroundings.

EN EL CASO DE LA DECORACIÓN URBANA, los espacios compartidos se delimitan a través de texturas diferentes o contrastes audaces, ampliando la paleta cromática. Se utiliza una ornamentación moderna y colorida que destaca en cada espacio y se permite utilizar materiales no convencionales y atrevidos, sin embargo, siempre cuidando la amplitud, la basta iluminación y la fusión con el entorno.

POUR DÉLIMITER LES ESPACES d'une pièce commune, la décoration urbaine opte pour tout type de textures et pour un contraste plus risqué, afin d'élargir la palette de couleurs. L'ornementation est moderne, aux couleurs vives et faite des matériaux inusuels et risqués. Cependant, la rentabilisation de l'espace, l'éclairage et la fusion avec la pièce restent importantes.

IM FALL STÄDTISCHER Einrichtungen werden Gemeinschaftsräume durch unterschiedliche Texturen und gewagte Kontraste einer breiten Farbpalette voneinander abgegrenzt. Mann kann eine moderne und farbenfrohe Dekoration verwenden, die in jedem Raum hervorsticht, genauso wie unkonventionelle und gewagte Materialien. Es sollte jedoch immer auf die Weite des Raumes, eine ausreichende Beleuchtung und die Vereinheitlichung mit der Umwelt geachtet werden.

shared spaces
ambientes compartidos
pièces communes
gemeinschaftsräume

THE AIM BY SHARING THE SPACE between kitchen and dining room, is to create a pleasant and spacious area but with distinct zones. A long bar with high chairs is the best alternative because it helps distinguish each space without interrupting the view—as well as the usefulness of having a breakfast bar which suits informal family life and keeps the dining room for special occasions.

AL COMPARTIR EL ESPACIO entre cocina y comedor, se busca que el ambiente sea agradable y amplio pero con las áreas bien delimitadas. Una barra larga con sillas altas resulta la mejor alternativa, ya que ayuda a distinguir cada espacio sin cortar la vista, además de la utilidad de contar con un desayunador, lo que favorece la convivencia familiar informal y permite conservar el comedor para ocasiones especiales.

LORSQUE DANS UNE MÊME PIÈCE nous avons la cuisine et la salle à manger, nous devons veiller à instaurer une atmosphère agréable et dégagée. Avec une claire délimitation de chacun des espaces. Un grand bar avec des tabourets est la meilleure option. Nous pouvons ainsi distinguer chacun des espaces sans gêner la vue. De plus, nous aurons un coin petit déjeuner, ce qui favorise la vie en famille, et nous pouvons réserver la salle à manger pour des grandes occasions.

WENN DIE KÜCHE und das Esszimmer aus einem einzigen Raum bestehen, sollte man darauf achten dass der Raum angenehm und weit ist, die beiden Bereiche aber voneinander abgetrennt werden. Eine lange Bar mit hohen Stühlen ist hier die beste Alternative, da hiermit beide Räume voneinander getrennt werden können, ohne dabei die Sicht zu versperren. Außerdem ist es sehr vorteilhaft einen Frühstückbereich zu haben, weil dieser das informelle familiäre Zusammenleben fördert und das Esszimmer für besondere Anlässe reserviert.

Transparent chairs are a delicate reminder of modernity in a setting framed primarily by timber. Together with the dense vegetation, the wall painted in purple provides a visual shock.

Las sillas transparentes son un delicado recordatorio de modernidad en un entorno enmarcado principalmente en maderas. Además de la basta vegetación, se aporta un choque visual con la pared pintada en morado.

Les chaises transparentes évoquent la modernité lorsque nous les disposons autour des meubles en bois. Une abondante végétation et un mur violet viendront provoquer un impact visuel.

Transparente Stühle sind eine zarte Erinnerung an die Moderne in einem Umfeld, was vor allem von Holz geprägt ist. Die Pflanzen sorgen außerdem für einen visuellen Bruch mit der violett gestrichenen Wand.

bars and dining tables
barras y comedores
bars et salles à manger
bars und esstische

THEY ARE DISTINGUISHED by being modern, bold, colorful and very original. Dining rooms and bars are designed to attract attention. The ornaments are large and showy. A variety of textures are used for chairs and benches including acrylic, velvet, velour, leather, canvas, ceramic, wood, stainless steel and metal. In general, the aim is to fill the space and generate a visual stimulus.

SE DISTINGUEN por ser modernos, audaces, coloridos y muy originales. Los comedores y barras están diseñados para llamar la atención. Los ornamentos son grandes y vistosos. Se utiliza una diversidad de texturas en sillas y bancos entre las que se encuentran acrílico, terciopelo, velour, piel, loneta, cerámica, madera acero inoxidable y metal. En general se apuesta por una saturación para generar mayor estímulo visual.

SONT MODERNES, audaces, colorés et authentiques. Les salles à manger et les bars ont été conçus pour attirer le regard. Les objets décoratifs doivent être grands et frappants. Pour les chaises et les tabourets nous pouvons utiliser une grande variété de textures : acrylique, velours, cuir, toile de coton, céramique, bois, acier inoxydable et métal. Il faut miser sur un stimulus visuel à travers de la saturation.

BARS UND ESSTISCHE zeichnen sich dadurch aus, dass sie modern, gewagt, bunt und sehr originell sind. Sie sind so konzipiert, dass sie Aufmerksamkeit erregen. Die Verzierungen sind groß und auffällig. Es werden eine Vielzahl von Mustern auf Stühlen und Bänken genutzt, einschließlich Acryl, Samt, Velours, Leder, Leinen, Keramik, Holz und Edelmetall. In der Regel versucht man eine gewisse Sättigung zu erreichen, um den visuellen Reiz zu erhöhen.

A broad, rustic wooden bar on a gray stone base with an opaque black background, naturally stands out to become the predominant image. It is complemented by metal benches that suggest modernity.

Una amplia barra de madera tratada rústicamente sobre una base de piedra gris, el fondo opaco en negro le permite destacar naturalmente convirtiéndose en la imagen predominante. La complementan unos bancos metálicos que sugieren modernidad.

Impossible de ne pas remarquer un bar en bois rustique sur une base en pierre grise et posé contre un fond noir. Avec des tabourets métalliques nous y apportons une touche moderne.

Eine breite rustikale Bar aus Holz auf einem Steinsockel. Der mattschwarze Hintergrund hebt sie natürlich hervor und stellt sie in den Mittelpunkt. Die Metallhocker wirken modern.

A simple dining table, either glass or wood, requires chairs that provide the decorative element. It is obvious they must be comfortable and ergonomic; however the variety of styles is very wide. Leather chairs in dark tones maintain a sober and elegant ambiance; if they are lined with fabric in an armchair shape they are very comfortable and relaxed for the diner, fostering a relaxed atmosphere; on the other hand, bench chairs add a touch of originality and breadth to the dining room.

Una mesa de comedor sencilla, ya sea de cristal o madera, requiere sillas que lleven el peso de la decoración. Resulta evidente que deberán ser cómodas y ergonómicas; sin embargo en estilos la variedad es muy amplia. Sillas de piel o cuero en tonos obscuros mantienen el ambiente sobrio y elegante; si son forradas de tela con forma tipo sillón resultan muy confortables y relajadas para el comensal, propiciando un ambiente distendido; las sillas tipo banca dan un toque de originalidad y amplitud al comedor.

Une table simple, en verre ou en bois, aura besoin de chaises pour contrecarrer cette décoration. Cela va sans dire qu'elles doivent être confortables et ergonomiques. Il existe une grande variété de styles. Les chaises en cuir aux couleurs foncées évoquent l'élégance et la sobriété. Si elles sont habillées en toile et ressemblent à un fauteuil, elles s'avèrent très confortables pour le convive, ce qui favorise une atmosphère détendue. Les tabourets apportent une touche d'authenticité et rentabilisent l'espace.

Ein einfacher Esstisch aus Glas oder Holz verlangt nach Stühlen, die das Hauptgewicht der Dekoration ausmachen. Sie müssen natürlich bequem und ergonomisch sein, allerdings ist die Vielfalt der Stile sehr breit gefächert. Lederstühle in dunklen Tönen sorgen für ein schlichtes und elegantes Ambiente. Wenn sie mit Stoff bezogen sind und die Form eines Sessels haben, sind sie in der Regel sehr bequem und sorgen für eine entspannte Atmosphäre. Hocker verleihen einen Hauch an Originalität und lassen den Esstisch breiter erscheinen.

The uniqueness of this space is that the room does not rely on the decor. It is the huge wall of glass with its reflections and glints, in conjunction with the lamp, that takes the breath away.

La singularidad de este espacio consiste en que el comedor no destaca en la decoración. Es el enorme muro de cristal con sus reflejos y destellos en conjunción con la lámpara lo que roba el aliento.

La particularité de cette pièce: la salle à manger n'en est pas la vedette, mais plutôt le grand mur en verre avec ses éclats et ses reflets, ainsi que cette lampe à couper le souffle.

Die Einzigartigkeit dieses Raumes besteht darin, dass der Esstisch nicht aus der Einrichtung hervorsticht. Die riesige Glaswand mit ihren glitzernden Spiegelungen raubt einem in Verbindung mit der Beleuchtung den Atem.

If surrounded by rustic timber, furniture with tubular metallic finishes can be chosen to merge two styles, combining warmth and modernity. To finish off the effect, a colorful and functional lamp can be added.

Si se cuenta con un entorno de maderas rústicas, puede elegirse mobiliario con acabados tubulares y metálicos para lograr fusionar dos estilos, combinando calidez y modernidad. Como remate visual puede añadirse una vistosa lámpara que resulte funcional.

Lorsque il y a des éléments en bois rustique, il faut choisir un mobilier avec des finitions tubulaires et métalliques, afin de fusionner deux styles différents. La modernité s'allie ainsi à la chaleureusité. Une lampe peut servir de marque visuelle, tout en restant fonctionnelle.

Wenn die Umgebung aus rustikalem Holz besteht, kann man Möbel aus Rohren und Metall-Lackierungen einsetzen und erreicht damit eine Fusion von zwei Stilen in denen Wärme und Modernität miteinander kombiniert werden. Als Blickfang kann eine große bunte Lampe dienen, die auch noch funktional ist.

THE SELECTION OF LIGHTING, striking and showy, directly influences the perception of a space. They may be chandeliers, hanging or standing lamps, but they all have something in common: they emphasize, decorate and embellish even the simplest room. The value of a lamp to decoration should not be underestimated, as they produce sensations of comfort, warmth, elegance and vivacity in any room.

LA SELECCIÓN DE LUMINARIAS, llamativas y vistosas, influye directamente en la percepción que se tiene del espacio. Pueden ser candelabros, lámparas colgantes o de pie; pero todas ellas tienen algo en común: destacan, decoran y embellecen hasta el comedor más sencillo. El valor de una lámpara en la decoración no debe ser menospreciado ya que provoca sensaciones perceptuales de confort, calidez, elegancia y vivacidad en cualquier habitación.

DES LUMINAIRES, grands et attrayants, vont influer sur la perception de l'espace. Nous pouvons choisir des lustres, les suspensions o les lampes sur pieds. Tous ces luminaires ont une chose en commun : mettre en avant, décorer et embellir la salle à manger la plus simple. Il ne faut jamais sous-estimer la valeur des luminaires, car ils apportent du confort, de la chaleur, de l'élégance et de la vitalité.

DIE AUSWAHL von schrillen und auffälligen Lampen hat einen direkten Einfluss auf die Wahrnehmung des Raums. Ob Kronleuchtern, Hängelampen oder Stehlampen, siealle haben eines gemeinsam: sie betonen, dekorieren und verschönern selbst das einfachsten Zimmer. Der Wert einer Lampe innerhalb der Dekoration sollte nicht unterschätzt werden, da sie das Empfinden von Komfort, Wärme, Eleganz und Lebendigkeit in jedem Raum bestimmen.

kitchens with islands
cocinas con isla
cuisines avec dessertes
küchen mit inseln

KITCHENS are characterized by their light tones, principally white tempered with touches of contrasting surfaces or appliances. In most cases the decoration is scarce, with empty areas and large closed cupboards that keep the surfaces free from utensils. The islands are spacious, elegant and practical with wooden, stainless steel, granite or marble surfaces.

LAS COCINAS se caracterizan por sus tonos claros, principalmente el blanco que se matiza con ligeros toques de contraste en cubiertas o electrodomésticos. En la mayoría de los casos su decoración es escasa, con amplios espacios vacíos y grandes gabinetes cerrados que permiten mantener las cubiertas sin utensilios. Las islas son amplias, elegantes y prácticas con cubiertas de madera, acero inoxidable, granito o mármol.

DES COULEURS CLAIRES, c'est l'une des caractéristiques des cuisines. Le blanc, en particulier, qui est contrasté par les couleurs de certaines surfaces ou quelques électroménagers. Dans la plupart de cas, la décoration est austère, l'espace est rentabilisé et les vitrines murales permettent de maintenir les surfaces sas ustensiles. Les dessertes sont grandes, élégantes et pratiques. Les recouvrements sont en bois, en acier inoxydable, en granit ou en marbre.

DIE KÜCHEN ZEICHNEN sich durch helle Farben aus, vor allem Weiß, das mit leichten Kontrasten auf Verkleidungen oder Küchengeräten abgestimmt wird. In den meisten Fällen ist ihre Dekoration schlicht, mit vielen freien Flächen und großen geschlossenen Küchenschränken, die es ermöglichen, die Ablagen frei zu halten. Die Inseln sind breit, elegant und praktisch mit Holz-, Edelstahl-, Granit- oder Marmorverkleidung.

THE ISLAND is marked out as the focal point of the décor in the kitchen by the visual shock produced by the completely white surroundings. A sense of refinement and order prevails in the space. The use of natural light entering through the large windows and flowing through the room is remarkable for its tonal range.

LA ISLA se distingue como punto focal de la decoración en la cocina, por el choque visual que produce al estar en un entorno totalmente blanco. Impera una sensación de pulcritud y orden en el lugar. Es destacable el aprovechamiento de la luz natural que penetra a través del amplio ventanal y que fluye por toda la estancia gracias a su tonalidad.

UNE DESSERTE est le point de contact de la décoration d'une cuisine, grâce à l'impact visuel qu'elle provoque lorsqu'elle est entourée d'un environnement blanc. L'hygiène et l'ordre y règnent. Une verrière permet une utilisation remarquable de la lumière naturelle. Grâce à elle, la lumière se répand dans toute la pièce.

DIE INSEL ist durch den visuellen Bruch, die sie in einer komplett weißen Umgebung hervorruft, der Mittelpunkt der Kücheneinrichtung. Es herrscht ein Eindruck von Sauberkeit und Ordnung in diesem Raum. Bemerkenswert ist der Einsatz von natürlichem Licht welches durch die großen Fenster fällt und durch den ganzen Raum fließt.

The island integrated into the breakfast bar is a highly functional concept that also allows it to be used as an ornamental tool. The tone of the wood used for the bar and the partitions exerts a warm and welcoming effect, standing out vividly from the spacious furnishings, with high gloss finishes in white. The stainless steel details of the extractor hood and oven merge in harmony to complement the comfortable atmosphere of refinement and order.

La isla integrada a la barra-desayunador es una idea altamente funcional que además permite utilizarla como herramienta ornamental. El tono de la madera en la barra y los muros divisorios ejerce un efecto cálido y amigable al destacarse vívidamente ante el espacioso mobiliario con acabados de alto brillo en blanco. Los detalles de acero inoxidable en la campana de extracción y el horno se fusionan en armonía para complementar el cómodo ambiente de limpieza y orden.

Il est très pratique d'intégrer une desserte comme coin petit déjeuner, car elle sert également d'objet décoratif. La couleur du bois au bar et les écrans apportent de la chaleur et se font remarquer face au mobilier blanc. Les détails en acier inoxydable des hottes et du four se fusionnent harmonieusement pour recréer une atmosphère confortable où règne l'ordre et l'hygiène.

Die Insel ist mit der Frühstücksbar verbunden, dies ist ein hochfunktionelles Konzept, das auch als Dekoration dienen kann. Der Farbton des Holzes der Bar und der Trennwände haben einen warmen und freundlichen Effekt, während diese sich lebendig von den geräumigen weiß lackierten Möbeln abheben. Edelstahldetails der Dunstabzugshaube und des Backofens verschmelzen harmonisch, um diese gemütliche Atmosphäre von Sauberkeit und Ordnung zu komplettieren.

The surfaces in high gloss beige or cream benefit from a visual shock of opposition in a dark color that unites the entire room.

Las cubiertas en tono beige o crema en acabado de alto brillo, se ven beneficiadas con un choque visual de oposición en color obscuro que enlaza toda la habitación.

Les surfaces en beige et avec un très haut contraste vont être compensées avec des couleurs foncées.

Die hochglanzlackierten beigen oder cremefarbenen Ablagen werden durch einen visuellen Bruch der gegensätzlichen dunklen Farbe, die den gesamten Raum vereinheitlicht, unterstrichen.

A pleasant island that incorporates a bar in natural wood. Modern benches provide a nice touch and stand out from the pale floor, reinforced by the dark color of the wall.

Agradable isla que combina una barra de madera natural. Los bancos modernos proporcionan alegría al entorno y se destacan sobre un piso claro reforzado por la pared obscura.

Une desserte très confortable avec une planche en bois naturel, et des tabourets modernes, apportent une touche de gaité. Ils se font remarquer grâce au sol en couleur claire et un mur sombre.

Eine angenehme Insel, die mit einer Bar aus natürlichem Holz kombiniert wird. Moderne Hocker erzeugen eine heitere Umgebung und werden durch einen hellen Boden und der dunkle Wand noch einmal hervorgehoben.

architectural arquitectónicos architectoniques architekten

65 *interior design project:* ESTUDIO 2.28, alejandra albarrán, mariana rivera

66-67 *architectural project:* EXTRACTO ARTE, ARQUITECTURA Y DISEÑO, vanessa patiño, robert duarte

68-69 *architectural project:* GRUPO ARQUITECTÓNICA, genaro nieto

70 *interior design project:* MATERIA, lucía soto, andrea flores

72-73 *architectural and interior design project:* ABAX / CABO DEVELOPMENT, fernando de haro, jesús fernández, omar fuentes, bertha figueroa, jorge torres

75-76 *architectural project:* MAYER HASBANI, mayer hasbani

76-77 *interior design project:* PAULINA JIMÉNEZ INTERIOR DESIGN, paulina jiménez lópez

78-79 *interior design project:* COVILHA, blanca gonzález, maribel gonzález, mely gonzález

80-81 *interior design project:* ESTUDIO 2.28, alejandra albarrán, mariana rivera

82-83 *interior design project:* ARQUITECTO AURELIO MAYO, aurelio mayo

84-85 *architectural project:* TALLER ESTILO ARQUITECTURA, víctor alejandro cruz domínguez, iván atahualpa hernández salazar, luis estrada aguilar

86-87 *architectural project:* DCPP ARQUITECTOS, pablo pérez palacios, alfonso de la concha rojas

88-89 *architectural project:* A CREATIVE PROCESS, andrés saavedra

90-91 *architectural project:* URIBE + ARQUITECTOS, oscar uribe

92-94 *interior design project:* BASCH ARQUITECTOS, alejandra bartlett, ingrid schjetnan

96-97 *architectural and interior design project:* STAINES ARQUITECTOS, carlos staines

98-99 *interior design project:* MARQCÓ, covadonga hernández

100-101 *architectural and interior design project:* ARQUIPLAN, bernardo hinojosa

102-103 *architectural and interior design project:* GA GRUPO ARQUITECTURA, daniel álvarez

104-105 *interior design project:* ELENA TALAVERA DISEÑO / G DEL CP ARQUITECTOS, elena talavera, óscar gonzález

106 *interior design project:* DIN INTERIORISMO, aurelio vázquez

107 *architectural and interior design project:* STAINES ARQUITECTOS, carlos staines

108-109 *architectural project:* BARDASANO ARQUITECTOS, enrique bardasano montaño, diego bardasano arizti, andrés bardasano arizti

110-111 *architectural and interior design project:* A.A.A ALMAZÁN ARQUITECTOS Y ASOCIADOS, guillermo almazán cueto, guillermo suárez almazán, dirk thurmer franssen

112-113 *interior design project:* INTERARQ, david penjos

114-115 *architectural project:* IX2 ARQUITECTURA, javier h. ituarte reynaud, javier h. ituarte landa

116-117 *architectural and interior design project:* H. PONCE ARQUITECTOS, henry ponce

119 *architectural and interior design project:* GA GRUPO ARQUITECTURA, daniel álvarez

120-121 *interior design project:* ESTUDIO ADÁN CÁRABES, adán cárabes

122-123 *interior design project:* CASA DARÍO, margarita solórzano

124-125 *architectural and interior design project:* ARQUIPLAN, bernardo hinojosa

126-127 *interior design project:* TERRÉS, javier valenzuela, fernando valenzuela

128-129 *interior design project:* LÓPEZ DUPLAN ARQUITECTOS, claudia lópez duplan

architectural arquitectónicos architectoniques architekten

198-199 *interior design project:* COVILHA, blanca gonzález, maribel gonzález, mely gonzález

200-201 *architectural and interior design project:* KABABIE ARQUITECTOS, elías kababie

202-203 *architectural and interior design project:* CIBRIAN ARQUITECTOS, fernando cibrian

204-205 *architectural and interior design project:* GA GRUPO ARQUITECTURA, daniel álvarez

206-207 *architectural project:* ARCHETONIC, jacobo micha mizrahi

208-209 *architectural project:* BELLI + LINARES ARQUITECTOS, maurizio belli, ricardo linares

210–211 *interior design project:* BASCH ARQUITECTOS, alejandra bartlett, ingrid schjetnan

212-213 *architectural project:* SERRANO MONJARAZ ARQUITECTOS, juan pablo serrano, rafael monjaraz

214-215 *interior design project:* BASCH ARQUITECTOS, alejandra bartlett, ingrid schjetnan

216-217 *architectural and interior design project:* PGM ARQUITECTURA, patricio garcía muriel

218 *architectural and interior design project:* CIBRIAN ARQUITECTOS, fernando cibrian

219 *architectural project:* GRUPO MM, carlos magaña valladares, mauricio magaña fernández

221 *interior design project:* STUDIO ROCA, rodrigo alegre, carlos acosta

222-223 *architectural and interior design project:* jorge hernández de la garza

224-225 *architectural project:* GLR ARQUITECTOS, gilberto l. rodríguez

226-227 *interior design project:* STUDIO ROCA, rodrigo alegre, carlos acosta

228-229 *architectural project:* BELLI + LINARES ARQUITECTOS, maurizio belli, ricardo linares

230-231 *architectural project:* JPC ARQUITECTOS, juan pablo pérez cervantes

231-233 *architectural and interior design project:* A.A.A ALMAZÁN ARQUITECTOS Y ASOCIADOS, guillermo almazán cueto, guillermo suárez almazán, dirk thurmer franssen

234-235 *architectural and interior design project:* A.A.A ALMAZÁN ARQUITECTOS Y ASOCIADOS, guillermo almazán cueto, guillermo suárez almazán, dirk thurmer franssen

236-237 *architectural project:* ARCO ARQUITECTURA CONTEMPORÁNEA, josé lew kirsch, bernardo lew kirsch

238-239 *architectural project:* ELÍAS RIZO ARQUITECTOS, elías rizo suárez, alejandro rizo suárez

240-241 *architectural project:* ARCHETONIC, jacobo micha mizrahi

242-243 *interior design project:* BASCH ARQUITECTOS, alejandra bartlett, ingrid schjetnan

244-245 *interior design project:* EOS MÉXICO, mauricio lara, sebastián lara

246-247 *architectural and interior design project:* GA GRUPO ARQUITECTURA, daniel álvarez

248-249 *architectural and interior design project:* KABABIE ARQUITECTOS, elías kababie

250 *architectural project:* BARDASANO ARQUITECTOS, enrique bardasano montaño, diego bardasano arizti, andrés bardasano arizti

251 *architectural and interior design project:* ATELIER ARS, alejandro guerrero gutiérrez y andrea soto morfín

252-253 *architectural and interior design project:* jorge hernández de la garza

254-255 *architectural project:* JUAN IGNACIO CASTIELLO ARQUITECTOS, juan ignacio castiello chávez

256-257 *architectural project:* EXTRACTO ARTE, ARQUITECTURA Y DISEÑO, vanessa patiño, robert duarte

photography fotográficos photographiques fotografen

akaash mora - pg. 70

alberto cáceres - pgs. 32-33, 84-85, 116-117, 138-139, 142-143

alberto moreno guzmán - pgs. 182-183

alessandro bo - pgs. 10 (right), 92-93, 210-211, 214-215, 242

alfonso de béjar - pgs. 48-49, 52-53, 120-121

amira prieto - pgs. 102-103, 119, 131

ana laura rascón - pgs. 146-147

ana paula ortega - pgs. 94, 168-169, 243

andrés gutiérrez - pgs. 11 (right), 27, 45

arturo chávez - pg. 106

arturo osorio - pgs. 40-41

carlos medina - pgs. 122-123

cecilia del olmo - pgs. 104-105, 150-151

derek dellekamp - pg. 10 (left)

enrique ayala - pgs. 4-5

felipe luna - pgs. 221, 226

francisco lubbert - pgs. 100-101, 124-125

francisco pérez arriaga - pgs. 230-231

francisco quesada - pg. 10 (right)

francisco varela - pgs. 176-177

frank lynen - pgs. 212-213

giorgio sabatini - pgs. 208-109, 228-229

gonzález ituarte estudio - pgs. 114-115, 170-171

héctor armando herrera - pgs. 34-35, 128-129

héctor velasco facio - pgs. 14-15, 18-19, 22-23, 28-31, 38, 44, 54-57, 68-69, 76, 78-79, 96-97, 98-99, 107, 108-109, 133, 145, 148-149, 152, 178-181, 184-185, 198-199, 202-205, 250

isaac cuéllar - pgs. 156-157

iván casillas - pg. 219

jaime navarro - pgs. 2, 132, 154-155, 173, 196-197, 200-201, 236-237, 248-249

jorge hernández de la garza - pgs. 194-195, 222-223, 246-247, 252-253

jorge silva - pgs. 46-47, 50-51, 65, 80-81, 140-141, 160-163, 167, 186

jorge taboada - pgs. 42, 190-193, 224-225

josé gonzález - pg. 218

leonardo palafox - pgs. 43, 58-59, 64, 88-89

leonardo walther - pgs. 20-21, 66-67, 256-257

luis gordoa - pgs. 188-189

marcos garcía - pgs 8, 11 (left), 164-165, 238-239, 244-245

mito covarrubias - pgs. 254-255

onnis luque - pgs. 24-25, 86-87, 251

paul czitrom - pgs. 16, 60-61, 74-75, 130, 134-137

pedro hiriart - pgs. 110-111, 232-235

rafael gamo - pgs. 174-175, 206-207, 240-241

rigoberto moreno - pgs. 36-37, 72-73

sandra pereznieto - pgs. 10 (left), 212-213

santiago mayo - pgs. 82-83

sofía felgueres - pgs. 112-113

tatiana mestre - pgs. 158-159, 216-217

troy campbell - pg. 9

verónica martínez - pgs. 126-127

yoshihiro koitani - pgs. 62-63, 90-91

Editado en Septiembre 2013. Impreso en China. El cuidado
de esta edición estuvo a cargo de AM Editores, S.A. de C.V.
Edited in September 2013. Printed in China. Published by
AM Editores, S.A. de C.V.